Scotland's leading educational publishers

Practice Papers for SQA Exams

National 5

French

© 2014 Leckie & Leckie Ltd
Cover © ink-tank and associates

001/31032014

10 9 8 7 6 5 4 3

ISBN 9780007504886

Published by
Leckie & Leckie Ltd
An imprint of HarperCollins*Publishers*
Westerhill Road, Bishopbriggs, Glasgow, G64 2QT
T: 0844 576 8126   F: 0844 576 8131
leckieandleckie@harpercollins.co.uk   www.leckieandleckie.co.uk

Special thanks to
Roda Morrison (copy edit); Donna Cole (proofread);
Marie Ollivier-Caudray (proofread); Ink Tank (cover design);
QBS (layout); Quentin Vidal (audio recordings);
Agathe Weiss (audio recordings)

A CIP Catalogue record for this book is available from the
British Library.

Acknowledgements
All images © Shutterstock.com

Whilst every effort has been made to trace the copyright holders,
in cases where this has been unsuccessful, or if any have
inadvertently been overlooked, the Publishers would gladly
receive any information enabling them to rectify any error or
omission at the first opportunity.

Introduction

The National 5 French exam tests the skills you have practised throughout the year – Reading, Listening and Writing – in the contexts that you will have covered in class, i.e. Society, Learning, Employability and Culture.

Speaking is also an important part of National 5 French, but you do not sit a Speaking test in May with the rest of your exams. Your final Speaking test will take place in school before the exam diet starts, probably sometime before Easter.

To do well in your final National 5 exam you need to make sure that you are familiar with the grammar and vocabulary you have been using in class. This book will provide practice for you in the sort of questions that you can expect in your exam. The worked answers will let you know what the correct answer is and also give some help as to how to answer the questions to get the best marks possible.

Each exam has two separate papers: a Reading and Writing exam and a Listening exam.

Reading and Writing exam

The Reading exam is made up of three separate passages. Each passage has questions that add up to 10 marks. The questions are to be answered in English. One of the passages will have an overall purpose question. This is a question that sums up the point of the passage. You have 1 hour and 30 minutes complete the Reading and Writing exam. When you are answering, think about spending around 20 minutes on each Reading passage.

This will leave 30 minutes to complete the Writing part of the exam.

The Writing question is always an application for a job. You have to write (in French) an email in reply to a job advert. There are six bullet points that you have to cover in your application. The first four are always the same and this means that you know most of what is coming up in the exam. The last two are different each year. As well as preparing what to write for the first four bullet points, try to prepare some structures that might come up for these last two as it will help you when you come to sit the exam.

You are allowed a dictionary for the Reading and Writing paper.

Listening exam

There are two different parts to the Listening exam. One is a monologue (one person speaking) and the other is a conversation. The monologue will have questions that add up to 8 marks and the conversation will have questions worth 12 marks. As in the Reading exam, there will be an overall purpose question. This will be one of the questions in the monologue. All your answers should be in English. The Listening exam will last around 20–25 minutes and you will hear each passage in French three times.

You are not allowed a dictionary for the Listening paper.

National 5 French practice papers

This book contains three Reading, three Writing and three Listening practice exam papers, which mirror the actual SQA exams as much as possible. The layout and question level are all similar to the exams that you will sit, so that you are familiar with what they will look like.

Audio tracks to accompany the listening exams can be downloaded, free, from the Leckie & Leckie website at www.leckieandleckie.co.uk/page/Resources

The practice papers can be used in two ways:

1. You can complete an entire practice paper as preparation for the final exam. If you would like to use the book in this way, you can either:
    a) complete the practice paper under exam-style conditions by setting yourself a time for each paper and answering it as well as possible without using any notes
    b) answer the practice paper questions as a revision exercise, using your notes to produce model answers.

2. You can use the **topic index** at the front of the book to find all the questions within the book that deal with a specific topic. This allows you to focus specifically on areas that you particularly want to revise or, if you are mid-way through your course, it lets you practise answering exam-style questions for just those topics you have studied.

All three of the practice papers in this book have answers to the Reading and Listening papers so that you can see what is expected for each question. There are also 'Hints' for each answer, which explain the answers in more detail. This is to help you understand where the answers are found in the Reading and Listening passages and what each question is testing. Look at these carefully as they will help you to understand what is expected of you when you sit your exam.

The following chapter of **Top exam tips** provides essential information on the Reading, Writing and Listening sections of the exam. These practical tips show you how to tackle certain question types, provide details of how marks are awarded and give advice on just what the examiners will be looking for. The section on the Writing exam is particularly detailed and includes a guide to how your writing will be marked, annotated examples of satisfactory answers and good answers and – lastly – structures that you can use in your writing. The structures are only a guide as to what type of information you should include. There are no set phrases when it comes to completing the Writing exam; the main emphasis should be on the quality of French used and its accuracy.

Top exam tips

The Reading exam

In the National 5 Reading exam, there will be three texts worth 10 marks each. You have to answer the questions in English. When you are given the paper, you should work through the three questions in order. They will be on different contexts you have covered in class – Society, Learning, Employability and Culture. The context that is not covered in the Reading paper will be the subject of the Listening exam. You are given 1 hour and 30 minutes for the Reading and Writing paper. You should try to complete the Reading questions in an hour, leaving 30 minutes for the Writing question. That means you have 20 minutes to answer each question.

Follow these steps to complete the paper and maximise your marks.

When you open your question paper:

- First read the information in English at the top of the question, as this will give you an idea of what the question is about.

- It is not usual for texts in the National 5 Reading exam to have a heading. However, if there is a heading, it will be in French. Work out what it means, as it will help you to understand what the question is about.

- Disregard the picture. Your answers will always come from the text – the picture is only to make it look nice!

- Skim read the passage.

- Skim read the questions.

Up to this point you should not have opened the dictionary! Remember, you have to answer the questions – not translate all of the passage.

When you start answering the questions:

- Don't start with the passage – start by looking at the questions in English.

- Look at each question in turn and mark where the answer can be found in the text, using a highlighter or underlining the relevant part of the text.

- Marking where each answer is cuts down on the amount of work you have to do. Most importantly, if there is a question you can't find the answer to it is often in any unmarked sections of the paper. This again helps you to pinpoint the relevant parts of the text and allows you to complete the paper with the highest mark.

- There are often clue words in the question (in English) that lead you to where the answer is (in French). These clue words are usually words that are similar in French and English, or they are words that should be familiar to you in French.

- Work out the meaning of the relevant part of the text to enable you to answer the question. Think about individual words, but also think about the sentence as a whole. You may be able to work out tricky words from the context of the sentence.

- It is only at this point that you should think about looking up any words you don't know in the dictionary. Remember to read the whole definition and choose the one that fits the answer best.

- When you are answering the questions, make sure that you put in as much detail as possible and that you actually answer the question.

- Stick to what the information in the text says – don't add in extra information you might know on the subject or draw conclusions from the information in the passage. You must write down what the answer is from the French in the passage.

When you have written your answers:

- Read them over to make sure that what you have written makes sense in English. The person marking your paper will always look for the positives in your answers, but they must be able to understand what you have written.

Mark any gaps you have in your answers so that you can go back to try to complete them when you are finished. It is easy to forget at the end of the paper that you have missed out a couple of questions. If you highlight them in some way – it could be by circling the numbers of the questions you have missed out – then you will remember to go over them as you look over your paper.

'What is the purpose?' question

- The last question in the last passage will ask you what the purpose of the passage was.

- You will have to choose from three options and tick the box you think gives the correct answer.

- This question is not designed to trick you but to make you think about what the purpose of the text you have just read was, i.e. why they were telling you about something. For example, was it aiming to help you find a part-time job or educate you about healthy eating?

For the whole Reading paper:

- Complete all three texts in the same way.

- Watch your timing. All three texts are the same length so you should split up your time evenly.

- If you are stuck on one individual question, or find one complete Reading passage difficult, move on and go back at the end.

- Don't forget that you have the Writing question to do once you have finished the Reading questions.

The Writing exam

For section 2 of the Reading and Writing paper you have to write an email of 120–150 words in French, applying for a job.

The Writing question is marked in a series of pegged marks. That means that there are set marks for different categories.

Very good	20 marks
Good	16 marks
Satisfactory	12 marks
Unsatisfactory	8 marks
Poor	4 marks
Very poor	0 marks

There is no set language that must be included in the Writing question to get the mark for each category – just broad guidelines as to what should be included.

The Writing question will be marked on three separate areas – **Content, Accuracy and Language**.

The first area that will probably be looked at is the **Content**. The person marking your Writing exam will read your answer to check that you have included information on all six bullet points that are listed in the question.

—   The first four bullet points, which are the same each year, must be covered in detail and accurately. These are: personal information, school experience, skills/interests, work experience/jobs.

—   For the two bullet points that are unpredictable, you must answer them fully. You do not need to go into a great deal of detail and you will get away with being less accurate, although if you make lots of mistakes or very serious mistakes this will affect your mark. Go for simple but accurate information.

—   To get top marks all bullet points must be covered evenly. Don't write loads for the first two bullet points and then less for the others. It gives the impression that you do not know all the details needed and are running out of steam.

—   To make sure that all six bullet points are covered evenly it is a good idea to plan your essay.

—   Take 5 minutes or so to work out what you are going to write for each point and stick to the plan.

—   The overall essay is 120–150 words so you should aim to write around 25–30 words in each section. This means writing probably only about two or three sentences for each point.

- You really should have an idea of what you will be writing for the first four bullet points before you go into the exam. You just need to make sure that you take the information you have worked on in class and make it relevant to the job advert in the exam.

- Use the plan to organise and make sure that you have not missed anything out. Sometimes people panic in an exam and they forget to put in information that is not only essential but they have already prepared. This can have an impact on your mark so take the time to sort out your essay before you start and keep referring to your plan as you are writing.

- Although you do not know the last two bullet points before the exam, they will be based on work that has been covered in class. Don't panic about these. Prepare sample answers in your plan.

- It is essential that you stick to verbs and vocabulary that you know for these last two bullet points. Don't rely on a dictionary. This may seem strange advice but this is when candidates start to write very poor quality French and this then has an effect on your final mark. Remember that you will only be writing a couple of sentences for each point so don't get carried away. The only time you should use a dictionary is to check spelling/gender, etc., not to plan complete sentences. The marker will be looking for accuracy and relevance. Don't show off unless you are sure of what you are writing.

Not only is it important to make sure you have the content correct, you must make sure that what you write is **Accurate**. This is the second area that will be looked at by the marker.

- If you have covered all the bullet points then the marker will look at the quality and accuracy of the verbs you use – the more accurate and varied, the better your grade. If you make a lot of mistakes with your verbs or use the same couple of verbs you will not get a good mark!

- Even if you make a few mistakes it will be possible to get 20/20 – very good. When looking at accuracy the marker will be looking at the quality of your language and how much in control of the language you are. A few spelling mistakes will be fine – any serious mistakes with verbs will mean that you will start to be penalised.

- As a rule of thumb, the better the quality of language you use, the less likely you are to be penalised for a few small errors.

If you cover all the bullet points and your verbs are accurate you have probably passed and the marker will then go on to look at other **Language** features you have used. This is the third area that will be looked at.

Language features you should include:

- adjectives

- adverbs

- time phrases – frequency

- prepositions

- conjunctions/linking words

- accurate spelling

Also:

- don't just stick to 'je' – use other personal pronouns ('on', 'il', etc.)

- avoid lists

Example: answering bullet point 1

Look at this example of a paragraph regarding your school experience until now.

> Je vais à Newtown High school. Je suis en cinquième. Je vais passer six examens de National 5 en maths, histoire, anglais, chimie, français et musique. Je voudrais passer trois Highers et je voudrais aller à l'université.

This would get you a satisfactory mark because it is mainly correct but very basic. Compare this to the sentences below, which tell you much the same thing.

> Je suis élève à Newtown High School. Je suis en cinquième donc je dois passer mes examens à la fin de l'année scolaire en juin. J'espère les réussir tous et bien sûr avec de bonnes notes parce que j'ai l'intention de continuer mes études au lycée l'année prochaine. Après avoir quitté l'école, je compte aller à l'université. J'aimerais aller à la fac à Édimbourg car je voudrais quitter la maison de mes parents et trouver un appartement avec des copains.

| This is still quite simple but is a better way of saying what school you go to. | This is a good conjunction to use to join the two parts of the sentence together. | 'Je dois' + infinitive is a good structure to use. It is easy to use but sounds quite complex. |

Je suis élève à Newtown High School. Je suis en cinquième donc je dois passer mes examens à la fin de l'année scolaire en juin.

This adds detail about when you will sit exams.

This phrase doesn't add to the meaning of the sentence but it makes it sound more natural and more French.

An adjective has been added.

This adds in a more detailed way of saying what you plan to do. . .

J'espère les réussir tous et bien sûr avec de bonnes notes parce que j'ai l'intention de continuer mes études au lycée l'année prochaine.

. . . and that you will stay on at school.

This is a good construction to use at National 5. 'Après avoir' + past participle is easy to learn but sounds complicated.

This varies from 'je pense' or 'je vais'. It is good to vary the verbs used.

This is another way to say to go to university. It is a shorter, more natural way. This shows you know both ways to say it.

Après avoir quitté l'école, je compte aller à l'université. J'aimerais aller à la fac à Édimbourg car je voudrais quitter la maison de mes parents et trouver un appartement avec des copains.

This adds extra information.

Examples of structures

The following structures are designed to help you with all the bullet points but are only a guideline; there are many more structures you can use.

Personal information

Je voudrais poser ma candidature pour le poste de ……………………………	I would like to apply for the position …………………………… **You need to start the email saying that you want to apply for the job. Read the advert carefully to make sure you apply for the correct job.**
Je m'appelle ……………………………	My name is ……………………………
J'ai …………………………… ans.	I am …………………………… years old.
J'habîte à …………………………… en Écosse.	I live in ……………… in Scotland.
…………………… est une grande/ petite ville dans le nord/sud/est/ouest de l'Écosse.	……………… is a big/small town in the north/south/east/west of Scotland. **There isn't much variety in what you say here – so make sure you don't make a simple mistake. Watch how you spell 'je m'appelle'. Make sure that you write your age as a word, not figures, and that you use 'ans' with age. You must put 'à' + town and 'en' + country (most countries) for where you live.**
J'habite à la campagne/en banlieue/dans un village.	I live in the country/in the suburbs/in a village.

J'aime mon quartier/mon village car il y a toujours quelque chose d'intéressant à faire ici et tous mes copains habitent près de chez moi.	I like my area/my village because there is always something interesting to do here and all my friends live near to me.
Je n'aime pas habiter ici car c'est trop tranquille et mes amis habitent loin de chez moi.	I don't like living here because it is too quiet and my friends live far away from my house.
Je suis + nationality Je viens de + country Ma famille vient de + country	I am + nationality I come from + country My family comes from + country
	The person marking will be able to see if you are male or female so get the masculine and feminine correct for nationality. This is good if you are not Scottish. You can say you live in Scotland but your nationality is different. You can then say where you or your family come from to explain this. Although it is not very complicated, it raises the quality of the French used.

School experience

Je vais à + name of school.	I go to + name of school.
C'est un bon lycée.	It is a good school.
C'est un lycée + adjective to describe it – mixte, sympa, excellent	It is a mixed/nice/excellent school.
Cette année, j'étudie	This year I am studying ....
J'ai choisi d'étudier	I chose to study ....
Je suis obligé d'étudier	I have to study ....
	Don't worry about putting all your subjects – a big list does not read well and although it won't lose you marks, it does not make a good impression.
Ma matière préférée, c'est .... car	My favourite subject is .... because
• le prof est sympa	• the teacher is nice

- le prof nous aide beaucoup

- je trouve que c'est une matière facile/ intéressante

- je m'entends bien avec mon prof

Je ne peux pas supporter .... car c'est très difficile/ennuyeux/ça ne m'intéresse pas du tout.

La matière que je n'aime pas c'est ....

Je m'intéresse beaucoup à .... donc j'ai décidé de l'étudier cette année.

Au lycée je fais partie d'un club de ....

Heureusement, la plupart de élèves de mon école sont sympas et ils travaillent dur.

Mon école a été rénovée il y a quelques années, et maintenant c'est plus grand et bien équipé.

Les cours commencent à neuf heures moins cinq et finissent vers trois heures dix, sauf le mercredi quand on a un cours de plus et qu' on qu'on finit à quatre heures.

Il est important d'étudier une langue étrangère parce que c'est très utile pour ma carrière.

En ce qui me concerne, il y a trop de devoirs à faire le soir et le week-end.

À mon école on est obligé de porter l'uniforme. Pour moi, c'est insupportable.

- the teacher helps a lot

- I find it an easy/interesting subject

- I get on well with my teacher

I can't stand .... because it is very difficult/boring/it doesn't interest me at all.

The subject that I don't like is ....

I am really interested in .... so I have decided to study it this year.

The sentences below give extra information about school. Choose a couple of sentences like these to put in your essay.

At school I am in a .... club.

Luckily, most of the pupils at my school are nice and work hard.

My school was renovated several years ago and now it is bigger and well equipped.

Lessons start at five to nine and finish at ten past three except Wednesday when we have an extra lesson and finish at four o'clock.

It is important to study a foreign language because it is very useful for my career.

For me there is too much homework to do in the evening and at the weekend.

At my school we have to wear uniform. I find it unbearable.

Je pense que l'uniforme n'est pas toujours très confortable.	I think that the uniform is not always very comfortable.
C'est une bonne idée car c'est moins cher.	It is a good idea because it is less expensive.

Skills/interests

Comme passe-temps j'aime + infinitive	As a hobby I like to ....
Dans mes heures de loisirs j'aime + infinitive	In my free time I like to ....
Mon passe-temps préféré est + noun	My favourite hobby is ....
Pour me distraire, je préfère + infinitive	As a hobby I like ....
	Mention a few hobbies
Je suis membre de l'équipe scolaire de foot/natation.	I am a member of the school football/ swim team.
Je sais jouer de + musical instrument et je fais partie de l'orchestre de mon école.	I know how to play .... and I am in the school orchestra.
Je joue au tennis.	I play tennis.
	Say when you do the hobby
le week-end/le samedi après-midi/le vendredi soir/une fois par semaine/par mois/tous les jours/pendant les vacances/ en été/quand il pleut.	at the weekend/Saturday afternoon/Friday evening/once a week/month/every day/ during the holidays/in summer/when it rains.
	Say where you do the hobby
au centre de loisirs/à la piscine/chez moi/à l'école/au parc.	at the sports centre/at the pool/at my house/at school/in the park.
	Finally, say what you think of it
C'est amusant/je le trouve très intéressant/ c'est passionnant/ça me maintient en forme.	It is amusing/I find it very interesting/it is fascinating/it keeps me fit.
	Try to use a sentence to link it to the job advert
Mon passe-temps m'a montré l'importance de travailler en équipe et de travailler dur.	My hobby showed me the importance of working as a team and working hard.

Puisque j'ai joué dans l'équipe de foot, je peux travailler avec les autres.	As I play in the football team I can work with others.
Avec tous mes passe-temps et mes études, je suis très organisé(e).	With all my hobbies and my studies I am very organised.

Work experience/jobs

	Write about work experience. Even if you have not done any – make it up. It is a good chance to use the perfect and imperfect tenses.
J'ai déjà fait un stage dans un garage/un bureau/une école/un restaurant pendant une semaine/une quinzaine.	I did my work experience in a garage/office/school/restaurant for a week/a fortnight.
J'ai travaillé comme	I worked as ....
Le patron était/mes collègues étaient + adjective	The boss/my colleagues were ....
Tout le monde était très accueillant.	Everybody was very welcoming.
Tous les jours, je devais classer des documents/servir les clients/répondre au téléphone.	Every day, I had to file documents/serve customers/answer the phone.
Mon stage m'a beaucoup plu/c'était une bonne expérience.	I liked my work experience a lot/it was a good experience.
Je n'ai pas du tout aimé mon stage/c'était ennuyeux.	I did not like my work experience at all/it was boring.
	It's also a good idea to talk about a part time job. Most students will not have a job, but you can make one up.
Depuis le début de l'année, j'ai un petit boulot.	Since the start of the year I have had a part time job.
J'aime mon petit job. J'aime travailler avec les gens/travailler en plein air.	I like my job. I like to work with people/to work in the fresh air.
Je déteste mon job parce que je n'aime pas travailler avec les enfants/les journées sont longues et ennuyeuses.	I hate my job because I don't like to work with children/the days are long and boring.

Je travaille dans un café le samedi et le dimanche/je livre des journaux tous les matins/soirs/je fais du baby-sitting pour mes voisins le week-end.	I work in a café on Saturday and Sunday/I deliver papers every morning/evening/I babysit for my neighbours at the weekends.
Le travail est bien/mal payé.	The work is well/badly paid.
Je gagne 6€ de l'heure. Ce n'est pas beaucoup mais au moins cela me fait de l'argent de poche.	I earn 6 euros an hour. It's not a lot but at least I have my own money.
J'aime gagner de l'argent parce que je peux m'acheter ce que je veux/je voudrais aller en vacances avec mes copains.	I like to earn money because I am able to buy what I want/I would like to go on holiday with my friends.

Although the wording may be different, possible areas that could come up for the other two bullet points include:

• **Request for information**

Je voudrais demander des renseignements sur ce poste.	I would like to ask for information about this position.
Je dois travailler combien d'heures par jour?	How many hours do I have to work a day?
Je commence à quelle heure le matin?	At what time do I start in the morning?
On gagne combien de l'heure?	How much would I earn an hour?
En quoi constitue le travail?	What do I have to do in the job?
Est-ce qu'il faut porter un uniforme?	Do I have to wear a uniform?

• **Reasons why you have applied for the job**

Je voudrais poser ma candidature pour ce poste car ………………………………..	I would like to apply for this job because ………………………………………………
J'aime le contact avec les autres.	I like to meet other people.
J'adore parler le français.	I love speaking French.
Je voudrais continuer à étudier les langues.	I would like to continue to study languages.
J'aimerais améliorer mon français.	I would like to improve my French.
Je voudrais travailler à l'étranger.	I would like to work abroad.

J'aimerais travailler comme	I would like to work as ....
Je suis très énergique/honnête/sincère.	I am very energetic/honest/sincere.

- **Describing a previous visit to France**

Il y a deux ans/l'année dernière, je suis allé(e) en France avec ma famille/en groupe scolaire.	Two years ago/last year/I went to France with my family/on a school trip.
J'ai passé une semaine extraordinaire.	I had a great week.
On a visité beaucoup de monuments. C'était un peu ennuyeux.	We visited lots of monuments. It was a bit boring.
On était logé dans une famille française/dans une auberge de jeunesse/dans un hôtel. C'était génial.	We stayed with a French family/in a youth hostel/a hotel. It was great.
J'ai goûté les spécialités de la région.	I tasted the specialities of the region.
Je suis allé(e) dans une école française. C'était très différent, mais je préfère les écoles en Écosse.	I went to a French school. It was very different but I prefer school in Scotland.

- **Previous experience you have that makes you suitable for the job**

Look carefully at this bullet point. If it comes up, write about your work experience for bullet point 3 and write about a part-time job here (or vice versa).

- **Your availability – when you can go for interview and start work**

Est-ce que je dois passer un entretien d'embauche?	Do I have to come for a job interview?
Je peux venir passer un entretien d'embauche si c'est nécessaire.	I can come for an interview if necessary.
Je peux commencer le travail fin juin.	I can start at the end of June.
Je ne peux pas commencer à travailler avant la fin du mois de juin car je suis toujours à l'école.	I am not able to start work before the end of June as I am still at school.
Je peux travailler tout l'été.	I would be able to work all summer.

Je peux venir en France pour passer un entretien d'embauche si vous voulez.	I can travel to France for an interview if you want.
Je ne peux pas venir en France pour passer un entretien d'embauche. On peut discuter au téléphone ou sur Skype.	I can't travel to France for an interview. We could speak on the phone or via Skype.

Linking phrases

heureusement	luckily/fortunately
malheureusement	unfortunately
cependant	however
donc	so/therefore
pourtant	however
c'est-à-dire	that is to say
en général	generally
néanmoins	nevertheless
surtout	above all
en plus	in addition
probablement	probably
de toute façon	anyway

It is a good idea to try to link together sentences in as many different ways as possible. The list here is just a few examples of words you could use. Don't overuse them but it will help your mark if you vary your sentence structure and don't just stick to simple sentences.

Marking guidance

This table gives you an idea of what is needed for a very good, a good and an unsatisfactory mark.

Very good: 20

How the question has been addressed	Mistakes made	Grammar and language features included
• All points answered evenly, including the last two bullet points. • Answers in sentences using a variety of structures. That means you need to use different verbs. You can't keep using the same structures. Where appropriate you should include different tenses. • The overall application should be planned and logical and read well.	• Although it is important to be accurate, you can still get full marks with a few minor errors. The important thing is that the mistakes are not serious. This means that you can have one or two wrong spellings or 'la' where it should be 'le' but when you start making mistakes with verbs you will not get full marks. • The more complex the language you use the more likely it is that a few small mistakes will be allowed.	• It is likely that each sentence will have a new verb and that a variety of tenses will be used. It is a good idea to use modal verbs – verbs like devoir, pouvoir. • Care should be taken to include adjectives and to make sure that they are in the correct position and agree with the noun. It is a good idea to try to include unusual or irregular adjectives as well as making sure that you use some adverbs and prepositions. • Sentences should be joined with a range of conjunctions. You can't just stick to 'et' (and) or 'puis' (then) – you need to have conjunctions like 'cependant' (however), 'puisque' (since), 'néanmoins' (nevertheless).

Good: 16

• All bullet points must be addressed but they do not have to be in as much detail, so can be a bit shorter and there can be a bit of repetition. • In this category the writing is still accurate, just a bit simpler. • All of the predicted bullet points must be addressed but one of the last two bullet points might not be completed at this level.	• Once again the verbs have to be correct. • Often a piece of writing moves from 20 marks to 16 because of the amount of small errors there are with spelling, adjectives not agreeing, mistakes with accents (or missing them out). • As with the category above, the more detailed your work is the more errors you can make. • You will be likely to lose fewer marks by making mistakes in the last two bullet points as they are not known before the exam.	• There is less variety in the language used and the sentences are not so complex. • The same verb can be used again (although there still has to be a reasonable range). • Sentences would normally be shorter and so fewer conjunctions used.

Unsatisfactory: 8

• The bullet points are not fully covered. One or perhaps both of the last two bullet points might not be completed in this category. • Sentences are less detailed and the language used is repetitive. • For the job application to be in the unsatisfactory category there may be a part of it that the marker finds difficult to understand.	• The most common reasons for writing being placed in this unsatisfactory category are the mistakes with the verbs used, both in terms of spelling and mistakes with tenses. • The errors in the writing cause confusion and make the meaning unclear.	• The sentences are basic and inaccurate. One or perhaps both of the last two bullet points might not be completed at this level. • Verbs used are limited and inaccurate. • The only accurate responses are for bullet points 1 and 2 about personal information. • There are examples of mother tongue interference, i.e. English words occasionally appear in the job application.

The Listening exam

In the National 5 Listening exam you are not allowed to use a dictionary, so to do well you need to learn as much vocabulary as you can. Practise listening as often as possible.

There will be two listening passages. The first will involve one person speaking and is worth 8 marks. The second will be a conversation between two people, with one person asking questions of the other. This passage is worth 12 marks.

Here are some things you need to remember to get the best marks:

• Read over the questions. Use the vocabulary you have learned to help you predict what answers might come up.

• You will hear each section three times. The first time you hear the passage, just listen and think about the questions. It may be difficult to stop yourself, but do not write. If you start to write you may miss part of the next answer and this can lead to confusion.

• When the passage has finished, make notes.

- On the second listening, look at the questions and write notes to fill in all the points of the questions.

- On the third listening, fill in any gaps in your answers.

- You do not need to answer in as much detail as you do in the Reading section of the exam – but, remember, you do not have a dictionary, so you need to know a great deal of vocabulary.

- This is worth repeating – to do well you need to know your vocabulary. You cannot know too many words and the main focus of your study should be on learning as much vocabulary as you can.

'What is the purpose?' question

- The last question in the first passage will ask you the purpose of the first person's monologue.

- You will have to choose from three options and tick the box you think gives the correct answer.

- This question is not designed to trick you, but to make you think about the purpose of the passage, i.e. why was the person telling you about something. For example, to encourage you to visit a particular country or to persuade you to eat healthy foods.

When you have answered all the questions as well as you can:

- Read over your answers to make sure they make sense.

- Check all your answers are in English. Any French (even if it is the correct answer) will not get any marks.

Topic Index

There are four different contexts in National 5 French. The questions in each paper cover all 4 contexts.

		Society	Employability	Learning	Culture
Paper A	**Reading**				
	Question 1	✓			
	Question 2			✓	
	Question 3		✓		
	Listening				✓
Paper B	**Reading**				
	Question 1			✓	
	Question 2				
	Question 3	✓			✓
	Listening		✓		
Paper C	**Reading**				
	Question 1		✓		
	Question 2	✓			
	Question 3				✓
	Listening			✓	

N5 Practice Papers for SQA Exams

You are given 1 hour and 30 minutes to finish this paper.

Total marks: 50

Section 1: Reading (30 marks)

Read the three texts and try to answer all of the questions.

Remember to answer in English.

Section 2: Writing (20 marks)

You can use a French dictionary for both the Reading and the Writing exams.

Leckie × Leckie

Scotland's leading educational publishers

Section 1: Reading (30 marks)

Text 1

While in France you read an article about a young person and his problems with the internet.

Aujourd'hui la plupart des gens ont accès à l'Internet très facilement – sur leur ordinateur ou sur leur téléphone portable. Mais certains pensent que ce n'est pas une bonne idée parce qu'on a créé une génération accro à l'Internet et aux jeux vidéos. Ça veut dire qu'ils sont dépendants.

Claude – 21 ans, chef cuisinier à Paris: «Il y a deux ans, j'avais un vrai problème avec les jeux vidéo. Je faisais des longues journées et je travaillais très dur au restaurant et c'était épuisant. Normalement, à la fin de la journée, on rentre chez soi tout de suite et on va au lit car on est crevé. Mais quand je rentrais à la maison, je ne me couchais pas. Dès que je rentrais dans mon appartement, j'allais sur l'ordinateur et je ne bougeais pas pendant toute la nuit car je jouais à des jeux sur l'Internet. Le lendemain j'étais très fatigué au restaurant et j'avais des difficultés à faire mon travail correctement. En plus, je ne sortais jamais avec mes copains et je ne voyais plus ma famille.

Tout a changé quand mon patron m'a presque renvoyé. Je me suis aperçu que mon boulot était plus important que les jeux vidéo et je me suis arrêté tout de suite.»

Questions

a. Why do people think that it is not a good idea to have easy access to the Internet?

1

_____

_____

b. What does Claude say about his days at work? Complete the sentence.

I worked long days and worked _____ at the restaurant and
it was _____

2

c. What should you normally do when you finish work?

2

_____

_____

d. What did Claude do as soon as he came home? Give two examples.

2

_____

_____

e. How did this affect his work?

2

_____

_____

f. When did things change? Give one example.

1

_____

_____

Total marks 10

Text 2

You then read this article about differences between school in France and in Scotland.

En Écosse, si on ne travaille pas à l'école, on risque d'avoir des mauvaises notes et des ennuis à la maison si les parents sont fâchés. En France, si on ne réussit pas à l'école, on risque le redoublement. Cela signifie que, à la rentrée, en septembre, on se retrouve dans une classe au même niveau que l'année précédente.

Imaginez la honte et la colère des parents si en juin leur enfant reçoit un bulletin scolaire sur lequel il est écrit qu'il est obligé de redoubler l'année scolaire. Le redoublement est officiellement présenté comme une chance supplémentaire, mais en réalité pour tout le monde cela représente une année ratée à l'école.

À seize ans, en France, on peut quitter l'école mais comme en Écosse beaucoup d'élèves continuent leurs études car ils veulent passer leur bac. À cause du redoublement, il y a des élèves de dix-neuf ou même vingt ans qui sont toujours au lycée.

En France, certains sont contre le redoublement, mais la plupart des gens pensent que c'est une bonne idée car cela incite les jeunes à travailler et surtout à réussir leurs examens.

Questions

a. What happens in Scotland if you don't work at school?

2

_____

_____

b. In France, what happens if you don't work at school?

1

_____

_____

c. Complete the sentence using the information in the passage.

Imagine the _____ and _____ of the parents if in June their

child receives _____ saying that they have to repeat a year.

3

d. How is repeating a year officially explained?

1

_____

_____

e. What does repeating a year mean to everybody?

1

_____

_____

f. Why do most of the population think having the risk of repeating a year is a good idea?

2

_____

_____

Total marks 10

Text 3

You then read this article about jobs.

Comment trouver un petit boulot?

- Tout d'abord, il faut préparer un CV contenant tous les détails nécessaires. Par exemple les détails personnels – ton nom, ton adresse, ton âge, mais aussi tes qualifications et les examens que tu vas passer. Le plus important, c'est la partie où tu décris tes intérêts, ce que tu aimes faire pendant ton temps libre. En lisant cela, un employeur peut savoir ce que tu aimes faire et cela va l'aider à décider si tu es le genre de personne qu'il veut employer.

- Puis tu dois envoyer le CV à toutes les entreprises, les magasins et les restaurants de ton quartier, mais il ne faut pas s'arrêter là. C'est une bonne idée de confirmer l'envoi de ton CV par un coup de téléphone et de persévérer. Cependant, pour trouver un petit boulot, le mieux c'est d'aller demander en personne dans les magasins ou les restaurants puisque c'est comme ça que les petites entreprises trouvent leurs employés.

- Enfin, il faut penser à tous les genres de petits boulots que tu peux trouver près de chez toi. Peut-être que tes voisins ont besoin d'un coup de main dans leur jardin. Y a-t-il des personnes de ta famille qui voudraient payer quelqu'un pour faire le ménage? Si tu aimes les enfants, tu pourrais passer une petite annonce pour voir s'il y a des familles dans le quartier qui ont besoin de quelqu'un pour garder leurs enfants.

Questions

a. What is the most important part of a CV?

1

_____

_____

b. Why is that important to an employer?

_____

_____

1

c. What should you do with your CV?

_____

_____

1

d. You should not stop there. What should you do?

_____

_____

1

e. What is the best way to find a job and why?

_____

_____

2

f. What kinds of jobs could you look for? Tick three box.

Do the garden for your neighbours	
Clean your neighbour's car	
Do housework for your relatives	
Do your neighbour's housework	
Advertise to wash cars	
Babysitting	

3

g. What is the article aimed at doing? Tick one box.

Helping you find a job	
Telling you what type of job is best	
Getting you to take a job working for your neighbours	

1

Total marks 10

Section 2: Writing (20 marks)

You see this job advertised and you decide to send an email to the company to apply for the post.

Hôtel du Parc à Lyon recherche un/une réceptionniste.

Vous devez avoir une excellente présentation, aimer le contact avec les autres et parler plusieurs langues étrangères.

Pour plus de détails ou si ce poste vous intéresse, contactez M. Martin à l'adresse électronique suivante: mmartinhotel@google.fr

---

When you prepare your application email, you must make sure that you include information from all of the following points:

- Personal information (name, age, where you live).

- Information about what you have experienced at school or college to the present day.

- Any skills/interests you have that make you the best candidate for the job.

- What work experience you have that would be relevant to the job you are applying for.

- Questions about what your duties will be and what your hours will be.

- Some details about a previous trip to France you have already made.

The email should be around 120–150 words long. You may use a French dictionary.

Practice
Papers for
SQA Exams

The Listening exam should take approximately 25 minutes.

Total marks: 20

You will hear two passages in French. You will have 1 minute to study the questions before you hear each passage.

The two passages are each repeated three times. There will be a pause of 1 minute between each repetition.

There will be a pause in which you can write your answers after each passage.

Remember to answer in English and write your answers in the spaces provided.

You are allowed to make notes as you listen but can only write on the exam paper.

You cannot use a French dictionary.

Scotland's leading educational publishers

Passage 1

Claire is talking about where she is living at the moment.

a. Why is she living in Senegal just now?

_____

_____

1

b. What is different about school?

_____

_____

1

c. (i) Why is their balcony so useful? Give one example.

_____

_____

1

   (ii) Why are they able to use it most of the year? Give one example.

_____

_____

1

d. What has Claire bought at the market? Complete the sentence.

At the market she bought _____ _____ and _____

2

e. What has she noticed that there is not a lot of at the market?

1

_____

_____

f. Why is Claire talking about this? Tick one box.

1

To tell you about her life in Dakar	
To tell you about her life in France	
To tell you about what you can do in Dakar	

Total marks | **8**

Passage 2

Julie asks her friend Guy about his holiday last year.

a. Why did Guy go to Quebec on holiday? Give two examples.

2

_____

_____

b. What did he do for the first week of his holiday? Give two examples.

2

_____

_____

c. What types of food did he try? Give three examples.

3

_____

_____

d. Where did he go in the second week? Tick one box.

1

His uncle took him to the lake by car	
His uncle took him to the mountains by car	
His uncle took him to visit his aunt by car	

e. What did he say about the journey? Give one example.

1

_____

_____

f. What new thing did he try there?

1

_____

_____

g. **(i)** What did he like most about his holiday?

1

_____

_____

(ii) Why?

1

_____

_____

Total marks 12

Practice Papers for SQA Exams

FRENCH

NATIONAL 5

Exam A

Listening transcript

The listening transcripts accompany the audio tracks, which can be downloaded, free, from the Leckie & Leckie website at www.leckieandleckie.co.uk/n5frenchpractice

Remember that listening transcripts will NOT be provided when you sit your final exam. They are printed here as an additional item to help you with your revision for the Listening exam.

Scotland's leading educational publishers

Listening Transcript: Passage 1

Claire is talking about where she is living at the moment.

Bonjour. Je m'appelle Claire. Je suis française mais en ce moment j'habite au Sénégal puisque mon père va travailler pendant un an dans le bureau de Dakar de l'entreprise pour laquelle il travaille. Dakar est la plus grande ville et aussi la capitale du pays.

Ma vie ici n'est pas si différente de ma vie en France. Je vais à une école au centre de la ville. Au lycée, j'étudie les mêmes matières et le règlement de l'école est presque le même que celui de mon école en France. Ce qui est différent au Sénégal pour moi, c'est qu'on est obligé de porter un uniforme scolaire.

Notre appartement se trouve dans un grand immeuble. On a un très grand balcon qu'on utilise comme salle de séjour et salle à manger. Le climat est très doux et il fait si chaud qu'on peut manger dehors sur le balcon toute l'année.

Comme en France, je vais souvent au marché avec mes parents et avec mes amis. Ici on peut acheter de tout – des fruits, des plantes et des animaux. Il y a aussi une grande variété de bracelets et de boucles d'oreilles. J'ai déjà acheté quelques T-shirts et un sac à main. J'ai remarqué qu'il n'y a pas beaucoup de chaussures au marché.

Ma famille et moi, nous devrons rentrer en France bientôt et je garderai de bons souvenirs de mon année à Dakar et je suis sûre que les couleurs vives du marché resteront mon meilleur souvenir.

Listening Transcript: Passage 2

Julie asks her friend Guy about his holiday last year.

Où es-tu allé en vacances l'année dernière?

L'année dernière, je suis allé au Québec au Canada. J'ai de la famille là-bas. Ma mère est née au Canada et j'ai voulu rendre visite à mes tantes et cousins qui habitent là-bas. C'était des vacances différentes et ça m'a fait très plaisir de voir ma famille. J'ai séjourné chez une tante et je suis allé voir mes oncles et mes cousins qui habitent dans le même quartier.

Qu'est-ce que tu as fait pendant ton séjour?

La première semaine, je suis resté dans la ville de Montréal, la ville principale de la région. C'est une ville historique et c'est très pittoresque. Il y a aussi beaucoup de choses à faire. J'ai adoré la vieille ville. J'ai passé un après-midi à faire les petits magasins dans les rues historiques. J'ai aussi visité les monuments intéressants dans la ville et le vieux port.

As-tu goûté la cuisine de la région ?

On est allé au restaurant plusieurs fois. En général j'ai mangé la cuisine française mais je suis allé aussi dans un restaurant chinois. Ce que j'ai préféré c'était de déjeuner au café. Les petits snacks au café étaient savoureux.

Et la deuxième semaine, qu'est-ce que tu as fait ?

La deuxième semaine, mon oncle nous a emmenés à la montagne en voiture. On a fait un long voyage. Le voyage a duré deux heures, mais le paysage était impressionnant. On a séjourné dans le chalet de ma tante. Je sais déjà faire du ski mais j'ai essayé de faire du snowboard pour la première fois. C'était tout à fait différent du ski mais cela m'a plu.

Qu'est-ce que tu as préféré pendant tes vacances ?

Pour moi ce que j'ai préféré c'était quand je suis allé à un match de hockey sur glace. Mes cousins sont passionnés par le hockey. Ils y jouent et ils adorent regarder les matchs aussi. C'était animé et très bruyant mais j'ai trouvé ça génial.

Practice Exam B

Practice
Papers for
SQA Exams

FRENCH
NATIONAL 5
Exam B
Reading and Writing

You are given 1 hour and 30 minutes to finish this paper.

Total marks: 50

Section 1: Reading (30 marks)

Read the three texts and try to answer all of the questions.

Remember to answer in English.

Section 2: Writing (20 marks)

You can use a French dictionary for both the Reading and the Writing exams.

Scotland's leading educational publishers

Section 1: Reading (30 marks)

Text 1

While you are in France you look at your French friend's school magazine where a pupil – Julie – gives her experiences of life in school.

Je suis en terminale au lycée en France et à la fin de l'année scolaire, je vais passer mes examens. Pendant toute ma scolarité, j'ai été une élève modèle. J'ai toujours fait mes devoirs quand il le fallait, jamais en retard, et j'ai bien préparé mes contrôles. D'habitude, j'avais de bonnes notes.

Cette année, j'ai continué à travailler. Mais tout est different, ce n'est pas si facile qu'avant. J'ai trouvé le travail en classe difficile à comprendre et je n'ai pas toujours très bien réussi. Heureusement, j'ai déjà passé mon examen de français l'année dernière, mais maintenant, au lieu des cours de français, il faut suivre des cours de philosophie. Ce n'est pas marrant!

Comme la plupart de mes amis, j'ai déjà commencé à préparer mon baccalauréat, que je passerai en juin, mais je m'inquiète pour les résultats. Je voudrais continuer mes études à la fac mais pour cela, je dois réussir tous mes examens et avec de bonnes notes.

Je rêve de l'été prochain. Plus d'études et plus de stress. Des semaines libres pour m'amuser et sortir avec des amis.

Questions

a. How was Julie a model pupil?

2

_____

_____

b. This year, what is different from previous years at school? Give two examples.

2

_____

_____

c. Why doesn't she study French anymore? Tick one box.

1

She sat the exam at the end of last year	
She didn't pick it	
She wasn't allowed to sit it	

d. What happens instead?

1

_____

_____

e. Why is she worried?

1

_____

_____

f. What does she have to do to continue her studies?

1

_____

_____

g. What is she dreaming of and why? Give two examples.

2

_____

_____

Total marks 10

Text 2

You then read about a pupil from the school's exchange partner school in Scotland who has written about her holidays in France.

L'année dernière, je suis allée en France pendant quinze jours. D'habitude, je vais en France pendant les vacances car j'ai de la famille qui habite là-bas. Normalement, j'y vais en août, mais cette année, ma famille et moi n'avons pas pu y aller car mon père devait travailler, donc on est parti début juillet. On a trouvé les vacances en juillet beaucoup plus agréables.

D'abord, à cette période-là, c'est beaucoup plus tranquille et calme. Bien sûr, il y a des touristes comme nous, mais la plupart des Français travaillent encore, donc il n'y a que des vacanciers. En août, il y a du monde partout.

L'une des meilleures choses c'était les festivités du Quatorze Juillet. C'est la fête nationale en France et il y a des célébrations partout dans le pays. Dans le village où je passe mes vacances, dans la journée, il y avait un grand marché et une foire le 14 juillet. Le soir, on a organisé un grand bal et un feu d'artifice. On a dansé, on a mangé et on s'est amusé.

L'année prochaine, on va retourner en France comme d'habitude et je vais persuader mes parents de partir à nouveau en juillet.

Questions

a. Why did she not go on holiday in August as normal?

1

_____

_____

MARKS
Do not
write in this
margin

b. Why was it quieter than usual?

2

_____

_____

c. What did they think of the celebrations for the 14th July?

1

_____

_____

d. What do they do to celebrate in the village during the day?

2

_____

_____

e. What activities were there in the evening? Tick two boxes.

2

There was a dance	
There were fireworks	
They had a bonfire	
They had a barbecue	
They played football	

f. What is going to happen about next year's holiday?

2

_____

_____

Total marks 10

Text 3

You then read this article from Pierre explaining about his lifestyle.

Pour moi, vivre sainement, c'est très important. Il y a quatre ans, j'étais très malade. Ça m'inquiétait beaucoup et pour cette raison je fais très attention à ce que je mange, et surtout à la qualité de la nourriture que j'achète.

Bien sûr, c'est important pour moi de garder la ligne, mais le plus important c'est de me tenir en bonne santé. Pour être en pleine forme, je fais de l'exercice plusieurs fois par semaine. D'habitude, au centre sportif, je fais de l'aérobic, mais aussi quelquefois de la natation et chez moi j'ai un vélo d'appartement et j'essaie d'en faire quand je ne peux pas aller à la gym.

Quant à la nourriture, je fais des efforts pour suivre un régime équilibré. Je mange au moins cinq portions de fruits et légumes par jour, mais je prépare aussi des repas variés et nourrissants et, bien sûr, sains. Comme ça, je reste en bonne santé.

Je ne mange jamais de fast-food. Je trouve cette nourriture mauvaise pour la santé et de toute façon, j'ai l'habitude de manger de la nourriture fraîche et simple et je n'aime ni le goût ni l'odeur de ce qu'on mange dans les fast-foods.

Questions

a. Why is it important for Pierre to eat healthily? Give two examples.

2

_____

_____

b. What does he do to keep fit?

3

| At the sports centre | |
| At home | |

c. What type of meals does he prepare?

2

_____

_____

d. Why does he not like fast food?

2

_____

_____

e. Why has Pierre written this article? Tick one box.

1

To warn you about eating an unhealthy diet	
To tell you to do more exercise	
To explain why it is important to him that he eats healthily	

Total marks **10**

Section 2: Writing (20 marks)

You see this job advertised and you decide to send an email to the café to apply for the post.

Café de la gare recherche serveur/serveuse.

Vous devez avoir le sens des responsabilités et être ouvert. Vous devez parler le français, l'anglais et une autre langue étrangère.

Pour plus de renseignements, contactez M. Dupont à l'adresse électronique suivante: mdupontcafel@google.fr

---

When you prepare your application email you must make sure that you include information from all of the following points:

* Personal information (name, age, where you live).

* Information about what you have experienced at school or college to the present day.

* Any skills/interests you have which make you the best candidate for the job.

* What work experience you have that would be relevant to the job you are applying for.

* Ask if accommodation is provided.

* Tell them about a school trip you have made to Paris.

The email should be around 120–150 words long. You may use a French dictionary.

Practice Papers for SQA Exams

The Listening exam should take approximately 25 minutes.

Total marks: 20

You will hear two passages in French. You will have 1 minute to study the questions before you hear each passage.

The two passages are each repeated three times. There will be a pause of 1 minute between each repetition.

There will be a pause in which you can write your answers after each passage.

Remember to answer in English and write your answers in the spaces provided.

You are allowed to make notes as you listen but can only write on the exam paper.

You cannot use a French dictionary.

Leckie×Leckie
Scotland's leading educational publishers

Passage 1

When in France you talk to Françoise about finding a job.

a. What is Françoise having to do to help her find a job?

1

_____

_____

b. What are the easy details to fill in? Give two examples.

2

_____

_____

c. What hobbies does she have?

2

_____

_____

d. What is the problem about filling in information about her ambitions?
Give one example.

1

_____

_____

MARKS
Do not
write in this
margin

e. Where is she going to send her CV?

1

_____

_____

f. What is Françoise mainly telling you about? Tick one box.

1

How to find a part time job	
Her search for a part time job	
What she wants to do in life	

Total marks 8

Passage 2

You then listen to a conversation between Pierre and his friend Philippe about his search for a job.

a. Why is he looking for a part time job? Give two examples.

2

_____

_____

b. What is important for him in a part time job?

2

_____

_____

c. Where is Pierre going to look for a job?

2

_____

_____

d. What hours would he like to work? Fill in the table.

2

During the summer	
When school goes back	

e. What is Pierre going to do with the money he earns?

2

_____

_____

f. What does Pierre want to work as later on? Give two examples.

2

_____

_____

Total marks 12

Practice Papers for SQA Exams

FRENCH
NATIONAL 5
Exam B
Listening transcript

The listening transcripts accompany the audio tracks, which can be downloaded, free, from the Leckie & Leckie website at www.leckieandleckie.co.uk/n5frenchpractice

Remember that listening transcripts will NOT be provided when you sit your final exam. They are printed here as an additional item to help you with your revision for the Listening exam.

Scotland's leading educational publishers

Listening Transcript: Passage 1

When in France you talk to Françoise about finding a job.

Je cherche un petit boulot en ce moment et pour ça je dois préparer mon CV. Au début, je croyais que ça serait très facile, mais maintenant que j'essaie de le faire, j'ai quelques difficultés.

Pour les informations personnelles, c'est facile. Ce n'est pas compliqué d'écrire son adresse et sa date de naissance. C'est également facile de noter ses résultats aux examens. J'ai tous les certificats. Les difficultés commencent quand je dois écrire ce que je fais pendant mon temps libre et c'est encore plus dur quand je dois parler de mes ambitions.

Bien sûr, je fais beaucoup de choses pendant mes heures de loisirs. Je vais à la piscine plusieurs fois par semaine, je fais même partie d'un club de natation – mais je n'ai jamais rien gagné. J'adore jouer aux échecs, mais chez moi avec mon père ou ma sœur. Je ne participe jamais aux tournois.

Quant à mes ambitions, il y a un problème. Je n'ai aucune idée de ce que je voudrais faire dans ma vie. Pour l'instant, je suis toujours au lycée et je pense rarement à l'avenir.

Puisque c'est nécessaire pour moi de trouver un petit boulot, je vais finir mon CV. Je voudrais envoyer mon CV aux restaurants et aux magasins de ma ville le plus tôt possible.

Listening Transcript: Passage 2

You then listen to a conversation between Pierre and his friend Philippe about his search for a job.

Pierre, tu cherches un petit boulot en ce moment?

Oui, maintenant que j'ai fini mes examens, je ne suis pas obligé d'étudier tous les week-ends et j'ai besoin d'un peu d'argent de poche pour financer mes loisirs.

Qu'est-ce que tu voudrais faire comme boulot?

Le plus important pour moi, c'est de trouver un emploi pas loin de chez moi et j'aimerais surtout travailler les week-ends plutôt que de travailler le soir.

Tu as déjà essayé de trouver un emploi?

Non, je vais commencer mes recherches ce week-end.

Tu vas chercher où?

D'abord, je vais me renseigner dans les cafés et les restaurants de la ville pour voir si je pourrais trouver un poste comme serveur.

Puis il y a quelques petits magasins dans le quartier historique. Je vais demander s'ils ont besoin d'un vendeur.

Tu voudrais travailler combien d'heures par semaine?

J'aimerais travailler à plein-temps pendant l'été, et si c'est possible, je voudrais travailler à mi-temps – le week-end ou après l'école après la rentrée en septembre.

Qu'est-ce que tu penses faire de ton argent

Je vais le dépenser un peu. Je voudrais m'acheter des vêtements et je devrais mettre un peu de côté pour mes vacances de ski en février.

Qu'est-ce que tu voudrais faire comme métier dans la vie?

Je ne sais pas encore. Je vais aller à la fac pour faire des études d'anglais et d'espagnol, et après, je vais travailler à l'étranger, peut-être en Amérique du Sud.

Practice Exam C

Practice Papers for SQA Exams

FRENCH

NATIONAL 5

Exam C

Reading and Writing

You are given 1 hour and 30 minutes to finish this paper.

Total marks: 50

Section 1: Reading (30 marks)

Read the three texts and try to answer all of the questions.

Remember to answer in English.

Section 2: Writing (20 marks)

You can use a French dictionary for both the Reading and the Writing exams.

Scotland's leading educational publishers

Section 1: Reading (30 marks)

Text 1

A French friend, Antoine, is telling you about his recent work experience placement.

Il y a quelques mois, j'ai fait un stage dans un garage de mon quartier, et par conséquent maintenant je suis certain que je voudrais être mécanicien. J'ai trouvé les journées longues, mais j'étais content d'y aller chaque jour. Je me levais tôt le matin car je faisais le trajet jusqu'au garage à pied. Je devais commencer à neuf heures du matin et je travaillais jusqu'à quatre heures de l'après-midi.

Je ne pouvais pas travailler sur les voitures tout seul, mais j'ai aidé les autres mécaniciens dans leur travail. En plus je lavais les voitures et je vérifiais les pneus. Un jour, je suis allé livrer une nouvelle voiture à un client.

La plupart du temps, j'étais dans le garage mais j'ai aussi travaillé dans le bureau. Là, je répondais au téléphone et je classais des documents. Les gens au bureau étaient sympa, mais les journées passaient plus vite à l'atelier.

Maintenant, à l'école, je fais beaucoup plus d'efforts pour mes études car je veux réussir tous mes examens. Je suis aussi en train de chercher un petit boulot dans un garage pour avoir un peu plus d'expérience. Je vais faire des efforts pour trouver un apprentissage quand je quitterai l'école.

Questions

a. How did Antoine's work experience help him?

1

_____

_____

b. How did he feel about his work experience? Give one example.

1

_____

_____

c. What were his duties during the day? Give three examples.

3

_____

_____

d. What were his duties in the office? Complete the sentence.

2

I also had to work in the office. There I _____

and I did the _____.

e. How are things different in school now?

2

_____

_____

f. How is he preparing for his future?

1

_____

_____

Total marks 10

Text 2

Antoine then tells you about when he moved to the town where he lives now.

Jusqu'à l'âge de dix ans, j'ai habité à la campagne avec mes parents. C'était une enfance idyllique. Je passais toute la journée dans la campagne autour de la maison avec les autres enfants du village – on jouait à cache-cache ou on se baignait dans la petite rivière. C'était très tranquille et il n'y avait pas de circulation ni de déchets par terre. En hiver, c'était un peu moins intéressant. Je restais à la maison et je m'ennuyais.

Mes parents ont décidé de déménager parce que mon père a trouvé un nouvel emploi en ville et c'était trop loin pour faire le trajet deux fois par jour matin et soir.

En ville, la vie était très différente. Tous mes copains habitaient pas loin de chez moi et je pouvais aller les voir tout le temps. Il y avait aussi beaucoup de choses à faire pendant notre temps libre. Je ne nageais plus dans la rivière, mais j'allais souvent à la piscine et je pouvais aller au cinéma facilement.

Au début, c'était difficile mais maintenant je n'entends plus la circulation et je ne remarque plus les déchets partout. Je préfère ma vie en ville, mais j'adore retourner à la campagne pour les vacances.

Questions

a. How does Antoine show his childhood was idyllic? Give two examples.

2

_____

_____

b. How was winter different? Give one example.

1

_____

_____

c. Why did his parents move house?

2

_____

_____

d. How was his life different? Tick three boxes.

3

His friends lived nearby	
He had a lot more friends	
He could see them all the time	
There were a lot of things to do in his spare time	
He went swimming in the river	

e. How have things changed for him? Give two examples.

2

_____

_____

Total marks 10

Text 3

Finally, Antoine tells you about a cruise.

L'année dernière, mes parents et moi, nous sommes allés faire une croisière. On a passé quinze jours sur un grand bateau. Au début, on a pris l'avion pour rejoindre les autres passagers à Cannes.

Une fois à bord, on c'était incroyable tout ce qu'il y avait sur le bateau. La cabine était luxueuse et spacieuse. Il y avait un cinéma, des salles de jeux, quelques piscines et une salle de musculation. On a vu des spectacles dans le théâtre et pendant la journée, des jeux et des activités étaient organisés pour les passagers de tous âges.

Tous les deux ou trois jours, le bateau faisait escale. Normalement nous descendions du bateau et nous visitions la ville la plus proche du port. Souvent on allait voir les monuments. Des fois, on allait dans les magasins pour acheter des cadeaux pour les copains et la famille. On était toujours content de retourner sur le bateau.

À vrai dire, c'était les meilleures vacances de ma vie et j'espère que mes parents organiseront des vacances en bateau pour l'été prochain.

Questions

a. Why did they take the plane at the start of their holiday?

1

_____

_____

b. What did they think of all there was to do when they first got on the boat?

1

_____

_____

c. What were some of the activities that could be done on the boat

besides the cinema? Give two examples.

2

_____

_____

d. What did they do when the boat stopped in port?

3

_____

_____

e. What did Antoine think of the holiday?

2

_____

_____

f. Why has Antoine written this article? Tick one box.

1

To advertise cruises	
To tell you about his holiday last year	
To warn you about going on a cruise	

Total marks 10

Section 2: Writing (20 marks)

You see this job advertised and you decide to send an email to the tourist information office to apply for the post.

> Le syndicat d'initiative de la ville de Lyon recherche un(e) guide touristique.
>
> Vous devez être organisé et avoir le sens des responsabilités. Vous devez parler plusieurs langues étrangères et aimer travailler avec le public.
>
> Pour plus de renseignements, contactez M. Legrand à l'adresse électronique suivante: mlegrand.syndicatd'initativel@google.fr

When you prepare your application email you must make sure that you include information from all of the following points:

- Personal information (name, age, where you live).

- Information about what you have experienced at school or college to the present day.

- Any skills/interests you have which make you the best candidate for the job.

- What work experience you have that would be relevant to the job you are applying for.

- Ask what hours you will work and how long the job will last.

- Tell them about a previous visit to France.

Use all of the above to help you write the email in French. The email should be approximately 120–150 words. You may use a French dictionary.

Practice Papers for SQA Exams

FRENCH
NATIONAL 5
Exam C
Listening

The Listening exam should take approximately 25 minutes.

Total marks: 20

You will hear two passages in French. You will have 1 minute to study the questions before you hear each passage.

The two passages are each repeated three times. There will be a pause of 1 minute between each repetition.

There will be a pause in which you can write your answers after each passage.

Remember to answer in English and write your answers in the spaces provided.

You are allowed to make notes as you listen but can only write on the exam paper.

You cannot use a French dictionary.

Scotland's leading educational publishers

Passage 1

Françoise tells you about her experience of going to secondary school in France.

a. Where did Françoise go to primary school?

2

_____

_____

b. When did things change?

1

_____

_____

c. Why did she have to spend the week staying at school?

1

_____

_____

d. When did she return home?

1

_____

_____

e. What did she do during the week? Give one example.

1

_____

_____

f. Why did it help her to be staying in school?

1

_____

_____

g. Why is Françoise telling you about this? Tick one box.

1

To tell you about boarding at school during the week in France	
To tell you about living in the country in France	
To tell you about school in France	

Total marks | **8**

Passage 2

You then hear your French friend Catherine ask another friend, Guillaume, about going to school in France.

a. What did Guillaume like about going to primary school? Give two examples.

2

_____

_____

b. What was different about his next school?

2

_____

_____

c. What was good about moving back to Paris?

2

_____

_____

d. Why was he happiest at lycée? Give two examples.

2

_____

_____

e. What does he want to do after school? Complete the sentence.

2

He wants to pass all his exams then _____ for two or three years and _____ a little.

f. Does he want to continue his studies?

1

_____

_____

g. What does he want to study? Give one example.

1

_____

_____

Total marks 12

Practice Papers for SQA Exams

FRENCH

NATIONAL 5

Exam C

Listening transcript

The listening transcripts accompany the audio tracks, which can be downloaded, free, from the Leckie & Leckie website at www.leckieandleckie.co.uk/n5frenchpractice

Remember that listening transcripts will NOT be provided when you sit your final exam. They are printed here as an additional item to help you with your revision for the Listening exam.

Leckie × Leckie

Scotland's leading educational publishers

Listening Transcript: Passage 1

Françoise tells you about her experience of going to secondary school in France.

Ma famille habite dans un village en pleine campagne. À l'âge de six ans, je suis allée à l'école primaire dans le village voisin et je prenais le car scolaire avec les autres enfants du village chaque matin et on rentrait à la fin de la journée à 5 heures. Mais quand je suis entrée au lycée, tout a changé.

Il n'y avait pas de lycée près de chez moi et j'ai été obligée d'aller passer la semaine en pension. Autrement dit, je ne rentrais pas chez moi le soir mais je restais à l'école pour manger et dormir. À midi, le samedi, après avoir passé la matinée au lycée, je prenais le car et je rentrais chez moi.

Pendant la semaine, j'allais au lycée et je faisais mes devoirs le soir à l'internat. Au lycée, je préparais mes examens et j'avais beaucoup de devoirs à faire, surtout en maths et en biologie. Si j'avais des difficultés en anglais, je pouvais facilement aller au cours de soutien à la fin de la journée.

Le week-end, je faisais mes devoirs mais je passais la plupart de mon temps à me reposer et je sortais avec mes copines qui habitent dans le village.

Listening Transcript: Passage 2

You then hear your French friend Catherine ask another friend, Guillaume, about going to school in France.

Qu'est-ce que tu as préféré, l'école primaire ou le lycée?

Je suis allé à l'école primaire à Paris. Je m'y plaisais beaucoup car j'avais de très bons professeurs et je m'entendais bien avec mes camarades de classe. La nourriture à la cantine était délicieuse. Le seul problème, c'était qu'on avait beaucoup de devoirs à faire.

C'était comme ça au collège?

Mes parents ont déménagé en Suisse et je suis allé au collège là-bas. C'était très différent de l'école en France. Nos matières comprenaient le français et les maths, mais aussi l'allemand et l'anglais.

Comment ça se passait au lycée?

Ma famille et moi, nous sommes rentrés en France quand j'avais quinze ans. J'ai retrouvé mes anciens copains. Je suis allé au lycée avec eux et j'étais très content d'être à nouveau à Paris.

Qu'est-ce que tu as préféré?

Ça, c'est facile. J'étais plus heureux au lycée car j'étudiais les matières que je voulais. Par ailleurs, j'aimais indépendant et j'avais beaucoup de travail mais je pouvais aussi sortir avec mes amis.

Qu'est-ce que tu penses faire après?

Je voudrais bien sûr réussir tous mes examens. D'abord, je voudrais travailler pendant deux ou trois ans et voyager un peu.

Et tu comptes poursuivre tes études?

Oui, mais pas tout de suite. Je voudrais attendre avant d'aller à la fac dans quelques années. Je ne sais pas encore ce que je veux faire dans la vie.

Answers to Practice Exams

Answers to Practice Exam A

Section 1: Reading – Answer Scheme (30 marks)

Text 1

a. Why do people think that it is not a good idea to have easy access to the Internet?   **1**

It has created a generation <u>addicted to/dependent</u> on the Internet and computer games. (1)

Clue words: Look for good idea – bonne idée

> **HINT**   You must show that you have understood **accro à** – this is a tricky phrase. Any word that gives the idea of addiction will get a mark. It will test your dictionary skills or you could work it out from the context. You don't have to mention 'Internet' to get the mark as it is already there in the question.
>
> You have to mention 'computer games' as it is linked to being addicted to the Internet. It isn't that complicated a phrase and so you will not get a separate mark for it.

b. What does Claude say about his days at work? Complete the sentence.   **2**

I worked long days and worked <u>hard</u> (1) at the restaurant and it was <u>exhausting</u> (1).

Clue words: Look for long and restaurant

> **HINT**   The underlined words are the answers. You can get a mark for another word but it must mean the same thing. If you are not sure about the adjectives – look them up. Make sure you are accurate in using the dictionary. You need to be exact about what words you use. The correct answer is 'exhausting' (or any similar adjective). 'Tiring' would not get a mark as it is not enough but 'very tiring' is ok as it is more like exhausting.

c. What should you normally do when you finish work?   **2**

Go home immediately (1)

and go to bed (1)

Clue word: Normally – normalement

> **HINT**   You must include 'immediately' to get the mark but words like 'straightaway/right away' are all ok. 'Go to bed' is a separate mark as you have already given enough information for the first mark. Just as some marks are tricky, others are quite straightforward and, if you get these correct, it can really boost your final mark.

d. What did Claude do as soon as he came home? Give two examples.   2

Didn't go to bed (1) AND/OR

Went on the computer and didn't move all night (1) AND/OR

Played video games (1)

Clue words: Either mais – but – or je rentrais – I returned

> **HINT** There are three answers and you can choose any two. You must have the idea that he stays on the computer all night.

e. How did this affect his work?   2

<u>Very</u> tired at the restaurant (1)

Difficulties in doing his work <u>properly/as he should</u> (1)

Clue words: Travail – work – or restaurant

> **HINT** You must mention 'very' to get the mark. Any suitable answer giving the idea of him doing his work as it should be done.

f. When did things change? Give one example.   1

He was <u>almost</u> sacked (1) OR

He realised his job was more important than video games (1)

Clue word: Changé – changed

> **HINT** You must mention 'almost' but any translation that gives the idea of losing his job is acceptable. It is important to write 'more important than'.

Total marks: 10

Text 2

a. What happens in Scotland if you don't work at school?   2

Risk having bad <u>marks</u> (1)

Problems with parents/angry parents (1)

Clue words: En Écosse – in Scotland

> **HINT** Be careful not to write 'notes' instead of 'marks'. You should have come across this word in class but often people make mistakes in exams.
> You will get a mark for either answer about 'parents' – but no more than 1 mark for this part of the answer.

b. In France what happens if you don't work at school?   **1**

You risk <u>repeating a year</u> (1)

Clue words: En France – in France

> **HINT**   The risk/**risque** part of the answer is not complicated. This answer is to check your understanding of **le redoublement** as this doesn't exist in English as one word. If you don't know the meaning of this word, be careful with the meaning of it in the dictionary. Remember the question is about school – this should help you find the correct meaning.

c. Complete the sentence using the information in the passage.   **3**

Imagine the <u>shame</u> (1) and <u>anger</u> (1) of the parents if in June their child receives

<u>a school report</u> (1) saying that they have to repeat a year.

Clue word: Imagine

> **HINT**   This question is not designed to trick you. If you know the English for the words you need, make sure that they make sense in the sentence in English. Read your answer. You can always check the words in the dictionary – read the whole definition to make sure that you have the correct meaning.

d. How is repeating a year officially explained?   **1**

An extra/another/a second chance (1)

Clue words: Officiellement – officially – or chance

> **HINT**   Any answer that gives the idea of a second chance would be accepted.

e. What does repeating a year mean to everybody?   **1**

It is a wasted year (1)

Clue word: Année – year

> **HINT**   A translation that gives the idea of 'wasted' or even 'ruined' would be accepted but not 'missed' or 'bad'. It is a question of reading the whole definition in the dictionary and checking that you choose the correct answer by reading your answer back.

f. Why do most of the population think having the risk of repeating a year is a good idea?   **2**

It helps motivate young people to work (1)

(Above all) to pass their exams/to succeed in their exams (1)

Clue word: Gens - people

> **HINT**
> As well as 'young people' you would get a mark for 'teenagers' but not for 'children' or 'youths'. You don't need to put in 'above all' to get the mark.
>
> Be careful about **réussir** if you have to look it up in the dictionary. Read through all the meanings carefully so that you get the correct one for this context – to succeed or pass exams.

Total marks: 10

Text 3

a. What is the most important part of a CV? 1

The section about your hobbies/your interests/what you like to do in your spare time (1)

Clue word: Important

> **HINT**
> There could be lots of different words you could use instead of hobbies – all of them will be ok as long as they are plural.

b. Why is that important to an employer? 1

It lets them know if you are <u>the kind of</u> person they want to employ (1)

Clue word: Personne – person

> **HINT**
> You must translate **le genre de** – the kind of.

c. What should you do with your CV? 1

Send it to <u>all</u> the businesses, shops and restaurants <u>in your area</u> (1)

Clue word: Tu dois – you should

> **HINT**
> It is important to answer in detail. This answer must include both 'all' and 'in your area'. The other words in the answer are easy to work out so don't throw marks away by not including detail.

d. You should not stop there. What should you do? 1

With a phone call (1)

Clue word: Suivre – to follow

> **HINT**
> Although this is a short answer, **un coup de** can be difficult to translate. This is where not only looking at the dictionary but thinking about the context of your answer will help. If there isn't an example in the dictionary, make sure that your answer makes sense in English.

e. **What is the best way to find a job and why?**   **2**

To go to the shops and restaurants in person (1)

It is how small businesses find their employees (1)

Clue word: Le mieux – the best

> *HINT*   This answer is straightforward but requires details to get both marks.

f. **What kinds of jobs could you look for? Tick three boxes.**   **3**

Do the garden for your neighbours	✓
Clean your neighbour's car	
Do housework for your relatives	✓
Do your neighbour's housework	
Advertise to wash cars	
Babysitting	✓

Clue words: Les genres de petits boulots – the kinds of jobs

> *HINT*   Only tick three boxes. If you tick one extra you will lose a mark and if you tick more than that you will get no marks at all.

g. **What is the article aimed at doing? Tick one box.**   **1**

Helping you find a part time job	✓
Telling you what type of job is best	
Getting you to take a job working for your neighbours	

> *HINT*   Read the whole article. Decide what the purpose of the article is. This question is straightforward and, although you need to think about the passage, there is usually one option you can disregard. Look at the other two and decide which would best sum up what the whole passage is about. Sometimes it helps to think which one would be the best title for the passage.

Total marks: 10

Listening – Answer Scheme (20 marks)

Passage 1

Claire is talking about where she is living at the moment.

a. Why is she living in Senegal just now?   **1**

Her father is working in the Dakar office (of the company he works for) (1) OR

Her father is working in an office there (1) OR

Her father is working there (1)

> **HINT**   Although the first answer is the fullest, most correct answer, in the Listening exam you
> don't need to have as much detail as you do in the Reading exam so all three answers would
> be acceptable.

b. What is different about school?   **1**

She has to wear school uniform (1)

> **HINT**   Listen out for **différent** – so that you can find what is different for her. The vocabulary for the
> answers is not too difficult but the skill is learning to pick out the correct answer from all the
> information.

c. (i) Why is their balcony so useful? Give one example.   **1**

It is used as a living room and their dining room (1) OR

It is very big (1)

> **HINT**   You only have to write one of these to get the mark.

(ii) Why are they able to use it most of the year? Give one example.   **1**

The climate is very mild (1) OR

It is so warm (1)

> **HINT**   You will have come across these weather phrases in class. You have to pick out **le climat** and this
> will let you know where the answer is. Even although the phrases are quite simple, there is a bit of
> detail required – putting in 'very' or 'so' in the answers.

d. What has Claire bought at the market? Complete the sentence.   **2**

At the market she bought <u>several/a few/some t-shirts</u> (1) and <u>a handbag</u> (1)

> **HINT**   Although filling in the blanks can be the easiest questions, you need to make sure that you listen
> to all of the details – you need to put in how many t-shirts and put down that it is a **hand**bag.

e. What has she noticed that there is not a lot of at the market? 1

There are not a lot of shoes at the market (1)

> *HINT* Think about your answer. Don't get confused between the words for shoes (**les chaussures**) and socks (**les chaussettes**).

f. Why is Claire talking about this? Tick one box. 1

To tell you about her life in Dakar	✓
To tell you about her life in France	
To tell you about what you can do in Dakar	

> *HINT* Listen to the whole article. Decide what the purpose of the article is. This question is straightforward and, although you need to think about the passage, there is usually one option you can disregard. Look at the other two and decide which would best sum up what the whole passage is about. Sometimes it helps to think which one would be the best title for the passage.

Total marks: 8

Passage 2

Julie asks her friend Guy about his holiday last year.

a. Why did Guy go to Quebec on holiday? Give two examples. 2

His mother was born in Canada (1) AND/OR

He has family that live there (1) AND/OR

He wanted to visit his aunts and cousins that live there (1)

> *HINT* All the answers are close together so be careful when you listen to pick up all the information you need. It is a good idea to listen and then take notes as you can miss information if you write when you are listening.

b. What did he do for the first week of his holiday? Give two examples. 2

He stayed in Montreal/the main town of the region (1) AND/OR

He spent an afternoon shopping (1) AND/OR

He visited interesting monuments (1) AND/OR

He visited the old port (1)

> *HINT* These are all phrases that you will have met in class. Read your answers when you have written them to check that you have all the details and that they make sense.

c. What types of food did he try? Give three examples.　　　　　**3**

He ate French food/French restaurant (1)

He went to a Chinese restaurant (1)

(tasty) snacks in a café/lunch in café (1)

> *HINT*　　Listen to the question Julie asks as that will help you pinpoint where the answer is.
> Although the passage does not mention a French restaurant you will get a mark, as the passage mentions French food and going to a restaurant.

d. Where did he go in the second week? Tick one box.　　　　　**1**

His uncle took him to the lake by car	
His uncle took him to the mountains by car	✓
His uncle took him to visit his aunt by car	

> *HINT*　　Listen for the word for 'second' – **deuxième** – to get the answer.

e. What did he say about the journey? Give one example.　　　　　**1**

The journey was long/it lasted 2 hours (1) OR

The countryside was impressive (1)

> *HINT*　　Listen for the clue – **voyage**. The answer follows on from it.

f. What new thing did he try there?　　　　　**1**

He tried snowboarding there (1)

> *HINT*　　This answer is very straightforward as the word 'snowboarding' is the same in French and English.

g. (i) What did he like most about his holiday?　　　　　**1**

He loved the ice hockey match most (1)

(ii) Why?　　　　　**1**

It was lively (1) OR

very noisy (1)

> *HINT*　　These are adjectives that you should have looked at in class.
> If you choose the second answer – noisy – then you must include 'very'.

Total marks: 12

Answers to Practice Exam B

Section 1: Reading – Answer Scheme (30 marks)

Text 1

a. How was Julie a model pupil? 2

She was never late with her homework/she always did her homework when she had to (1)

She studied well for her tests/she usually got good marks (1)

Clue words: Une élève modèle – a model pupil

> **HINT**
>
> **Devoirs** is a phrase you should be used to from class work. This question is to test if you can recognise the negative **jamais** and the phrase **en retard**.
>
> Be careful with **contrôles** – this verb trips a lot of people up. If you have not met this in class think what the question is about to help you when you look in the dictionary as there are many different meanings.

b. This year, what is different from previous years at school? Give two examples. 2

It's not so easy (1) AND/OR

She finds the work in class difficult to understand (1) AND/OR

She doesn't always do (very) well/pass (very) well (1)

Clue word: Avant – before (this isn't as obvious as other clue words)

> **HINT**
>
> The first answer isn't complicated but it comes before the clue word so it isn't obvious that it is the word you are looking for.
>
> The second mark is more straightforward. This is to check your understanding of **réussi**. When the answer is in brackets you do not have to write it down to get the mark so although **très** is in the passage you do not need all the details to get the mark. Working out **réussi** is difficult enough on its own.

c. Why doesn't she study French anymore? Tick one box. 1

She sat the exam at the end of last year	✓
She didn't pick it	
She wasn't allowed to sit it	

Clue words: J'ai déjà passé – I have already sat

> **HINT**
>
> Look at the French in the passage to get your answer – don't guess. Look for words that you know will give you a clue as to which one is correct.

d. What happens instead? 1

She studies philosophy/she takes philosophy lessons (1)

Clue words: Au lieu de – in place of/instead of

> **HINT** The subject she is studying is easy to get but be careful about **suivre** – you will not get a mark if you say 'follow' as we do not say this in English. This is an example of where you need to read over your answer carefully to make sure that it makes sense in English.

e. Why is she worried? 1

She is worried about the results (1)

> **HINT** This is to test if you can understand the reflexive verb **je m'inquiète** and to see if you can pick out the correct answer from part of a sentence. The answer itself is not difficult but you have to work out the whole sentence or the reflexive verb to find out which part is relevant.

f. What does she have to do to continue her studies? 1

She has to pass all her exams with good marks (1)

Clue words: Je voudrais continuer – I would like to continue

> **HINT** This question is to test both the understanding of **réussir** and **notes**. They can have different meanings in different contexts and this can be confusing. You should have come across these when preparing for your exam – but read over your answer to make sure that it makes sense.

g. What is she dreaming of and why? Give two examples. 2

Next summer (1) AND/OR

No more stress/studying (1) AND/OR

Weeks free to enjoy herself and go out with friends (1)

Clue words: Je rêve – I am dreaming

> **HINT** **L'été** can be confusing. If you have to look it up make sure you are using the noun – summer – and not the verb – was. **Plus de** is another phrase that can mean several things.
>
> There is more information required for the second mark but it is straightforward and the vocabulary should be familiar.

Total marks: 10

Text 2

a. Why did she not go on holiday in August as normal?   **1**

Her father had to work (1)

Clue word: Mais – but

> **HINT** Most of the vocabulary is not difficult for the answer but there is a lot of information to work through to get to it. Watch the verb **devait** – but you will get the mark even if you put the answer in the wrong tense, e.g. if you say 'he has to work'.

b. Why was it quieter than usual?   **2**

Most of the French people were <u>still</u> working (1)

There were <u>only</u> holidaymakers/tourists there (1)

Clue word: Tranquille – calm

> **HINT** It is important that you include **encore** – 'still' – in your answer to get the mark.
> There were 'only' the holidaymakers. The most important part of this is to make sure that you translate the negative **ne … que** – 'only' – correctly. This can be tricky.

c. What did they think of the celebrations for the 14th July?   **1**

They were one of the best things (about the holiday) (1)

Clue words: Du Quatorze Juillet

d. What do they do to celebrate in the village during the day?   **2**

There was a big market (1)

There was a fair/carnival (1)

Clue words: Dans la journée

> **HINT** The answers are not complicated but you must make sure that you only include the celebrations during the day.

e. What activities were there in the evening? Tick two boxes.   **2**

There was a dance	✓
There were fireworks	✓
They had a bonfire	
They had a barbecue	
They played football	

Clue words: Le soir

f. What is going to happen about next year's holiday? **2**

They are going to return to France <u>as usual</u> (1)

They are going to persuade their parents to go <u>again</u> in July (1)

Clue words: L'année prochaine

> *HINT* It is important here to include **comme d'habitude** – 'as usual'.
> Make sure that your answer includes 'again' – **à nouveau.**

Total marks: 10

Text 3

a. Why is it important for Pierre to eat healthily? Give two examples. **2**

Four years ago he was very ill (1) AND/OR

It worried him a lot (1) AND/OR

So he pays attention to what he eats/the quality of the food he buys (1)

Clue words: Je mange – I eat

> *HINT* There are three answers but you only have to choose two.
> The first answer is to make sure that you understand the phrase **il y a quatre ans**.
> In the third answer the alternatives given are very similar so you will only get a mark for either, not both of them.

b. What does he do to keep fit? **3**

At the sports centre	aerobics, swimming
At home	exercise bike

Clue words: Je fais de l'exercice – I do exercise

> *HINT* This is a straightforward question. Make sure that you work out which sports go with which location and don't throw away marks.

c. What kind of meals does he prepare? **2**

Varied (1), nourishing (1) and healthy (1)

Clue words: Je prépare aussi des repas – I also prepare meals

> **HINT** The answer is straightforward. You should identify two of the three adjectives, but there is a lot of information around them and you have to read through several sentences to find the correct words.

d. Why does he not like fast food? 2

It is unhealthy (1) AND/OR

He is used to eating fresh and simple food (1) AND/OR

He doesn't like the taste or the smell of fast food (1)

Clue word: Des repas – meals

> **HINT** The clue word **fast-food** is easy to find as it is a cognate (like the English word).
> **Fraîche** – the feminine of fresh is used.
> The third answer is to check that you understand **ne … ni … ni …** (neither/nor)

e. Why has Pierre written this article? Tick one box. 1

To warn you about eating an unhealthy diet	
To tell you to do more exercise	
To explain why it is important to him that he eats healthily	✓

> **HINT** Read the whole article. Decide what the purpose of the article is. This question is straightforward and, although you need to think about the passage, there is usually one option you can disregard. Look at the other two and decide which would best sum up what the whole passage is about. Sometimes it helps to think which one would be the best title for the passage.

Total marks: 10

Listening – Answer Scheme (20 marks)

Passage 1

When in France you talk to Françoise about finding a job.

a. What is Françoise having to do to help her find a job? 1

She has to make up a CV (1)

> **HINT** Listen for 'CV' – if you can pick out this word then it is easy to work out the answer as it is the same as in English. If you can't pick it out you can use the next answer to work out what is being prepared.

b. What are the easy details to fill in? Give two examples.   **2**

Personal details (1) AND/OR

Name and address (1) AND/OR

Date of birth (1)

> **HINT**   This is information that should be familiar to you. You need to listen for words that you know the first time you hear them, and then use your common sense to fill in any points you have missed.

c. What hobbies does she have?   **2**

Swimming/in swimming club (1)

Playing chess (at home with dad or sister) (1)

> **HINT**   Listen out for the word 'club' and then use that to listen for hobbies that you know. You just need to write down the hobbies – you don't have to pick out where they do the hobby.

d. What is the problem about filling in information about her ambitions? Give one example.   **1**

She doesn't know what she wants to do in life/in the future (1) OR

She rarely thinks/doesn't think about the future (at the moment) (1)

> **HINT**   Listen for the word 'problem'; this will guide you to the correct answer. The French and English are very similar. You don't have to translate the French exactly into English as long as you answer the question.

e. Where is she going to send her CV?   **1**

Restaurants and shops in her town (1)

> **HINT**   When you see 'send' in the question, think about the French for it – **envoyer** – and use that to listen for the answer. If you don't know the word, pick out what you can understand from the last part of the passage.

f. What is Françoise mainly telling you about? Tick one box.   **1**

How to find a part time job	
Her search for a part time job	✓
What she wants to do in life	

HINT Listen to the whole article. Decide what the purpose of the article is. This question is straightforward and, although you need to think about the passage, there is usually one option you can disregard. Look at the other two and decide which would best sum up what the whole passage is about. Sometimes it helps to think which one would be the best title for the passage.

Total marks: 8

Passage 2

You then listen to a conversation between Pierre and his friend Philippe about his search for a job.

a. Why is he looking for a part time job? Give two examples. 2

He has finished his exams (1) AND/OR

He doesn't have to study every weekend (1) AND/OR

Needs money (1)

HINT There are three answers but you only need to give two. For each mark there is a word that should be familiar. This should make it easy to work out where the answer is and what it is.

b. What is important for him in a part time job? 2

Find a job not far from his house (1)

He would prefer to work weekends (rather than in the evening) (1)

HINT Although the words are not difficult, the answer is quite tricky as you have to listen for **pas loin** – 'not far' – and not be confused by **plutôt que** – 'rather than'.

It is also important to translate **chez moi** correctly.

c. Where is Pierre going to look for a job? 2

(Firstly) he is going to ask in cafés and restaurants in his town/the town where he lives/to see if he can find a job/position as a waiter (1)

(Then) he is going ask in the (small) shops/boutiques (in the old area of town) to see if they need a (shop) assistant (1)

HINT Although there is a lot of detail in the passage, you don't need to have all the details in the answer. You must make sure, however, that you don't put in wrong details as then you will not get the mark.

d. What hours would he like to work? Fill in the table.   2

During the summer	full time
When school goes back	part time the weekends/after school

> **HINT**   Although you should recognise the words for 'summer' – **l'été** – and when school goes back – **la rentrée** – you have to listen carefully to pick out 'full time' and 'part time'. For the second mark you do have the option of 'the weekend' or 'after school', which are words you should have met more often in class.

e. What is Pierre going to do with the money he earns?   2

Buy some clothes (1)

Save for a (ski) holiday (in February) (1)

> **HINT**   You should be able to predict that he will be buying something and you can use the context to listen out for the phrase for 'saving money'.

f. What does Pierre want to work as later on? Give two examples.   2

He doesn't know (1) AND/OR

Going to go to university/going to study English and Spanish (1) AND/OR

Going to work abroad/to South America (1)

> **HINT**   When you read the question it should make you think of all the vocabulary you have studied about future plans. Be careful of **travailler** – remember it means 'to work', not 'to travel'. In an exam situation, students often get confused.

Total marks: 12

Answers to Practice Exam C

Section 1: Reading – Answer Scheme (30 marks)

Text 1

a. How did his Antoine's experience help him? 1

He did his work experience in a garage and now he is sure he wants to be a mechanic

Clue words: J'ai fait un stage – I did a work experience placement

> **HINT** Although this answer is easily found in the passage, you need both parts to get the mark.

b. How did he feel about his work experience? Give one example. 1

The days were long (1) AND/OR

He was happy to go (there each day) (1)

Clue word: J'ai trouvé – I found

> **HINT** The question is straightforward and the words are ones that you should have met in class. You only need one piece of information as there is only one mark available.
> Although you don't need it for the answer it will help your understanding if you know **y** – 'there'.

c. What were his duties during the day? Give three examples. 3

He couldn't work on the cars alone/helped the mechanics with their work (1) AND/OR

Washed the cars (1) AND/OR

Checked the tyres (1) AND/OR

Delivered a new car to a customer (1)

Clue word: Travailler – to work

> **HINT** There is a range of answers and you only need to get three out of the four. Although the vocabulary is about cars, even if you have not looked at this type of job in class, you will have met most of the vocabulary in other contexts. When you look at the passage go with what you think the answer is and check anything you are not sure about in the dictionary.

d. What were his duties in the office? Complete the sentence.   2

There I <u>had to answer the phone</u> (1) and I did the <u>filing/filed documents</u>. (1)

Clue words: J'ai aussi travaillé dans le bureau

> **HINT**   **Je classais des documents** could be a phrase that you have not yet met. This can be checked in the dictionary.
> Remember that you will have to look up the verb in the dictionary in the infinitive form – **classer** – 'to file'.

e. How are things different in school now?   2

He makes much more of an effort (1)

He wants to pass all his exams (1)

Clue words: Maintenant, à l'école – now at school

> **HINT**   The question is to check your understanding of **plus de** – 'more'. Make sure that you translate **réussir** correctly as it has several meanings.

f. How is he preparing for his future?   1

Looking for a <u>part time/casual job</u> to have a bit <u>more experience</u> (1)

Clue word: Chercher – to look for

> **HINT**   You need to show that you have understood **un petit boulot** – 'a part time/casual job' and that you put the detail – 'a little more experience' – **un peu plus**.

Total marks: 10

Text 2

a. How does Antoine show his childhood was idyllic? Give two examples.   2

He spent all day in the countryside (around his house) with the other children (in the village) (1) AND/OR

He played at hide and seek (1) AND/OR

He bathed/swam in the small river (1)

Clue words: Une enfance idyllique – an idyllic childhood

> **HINT**   Most of the information for the answers is not complicated and you do not need to put in all the details. You may not have met the phrase **jouait à cache-cache** before but it will be in the dictionary. Make sure you think about the question before you look it up to get the correct meaning for the context. Depending on the dictionary you might get the answer from just **cache-cache**. If you need to use **jouait** – remember you will have to look up the infinitive – **jouer**.

b. How was winter different? Give one example.   **1**

It was less interesting (1) AND/OR

He stayed at home (1) AND/OR

He was bored (1)

Clue words: En hiver – in winter

> *HINT*   It is important to include **moins** – 'less'.

c. Why did his parents move house?   **2**

His father found a new job in town (1)

It was too far to travel twice a day (1)

Clue word: Déménager – to move house

> *HINT*   You must make sure that you include **trop** – 'too' – in your answer.

d. How was his life different? Tick three boxes.   **3**

His friends lived nearby	✓
He had a lot more friends	
He could see them all the time	✓
There were a lot of things to do in his spare time	✓
He went swimming in the river	

Clue word: Différente – different

> *HINT*   Although the answers are not complicated, be careful when you answer these. Some of the information in the options that are wrong are in the passage. Make sure that you look at the details for the answers you choose.

e. How have things changed for him? Give two examples.   **2**

He doesn't hear the traffic any more (1) AND/OR

He doesn't notice the litter everywhere (1) AND/OR

He prefers his life in town (1)

> *HINT*   The negative **ne ... plus** – 'no longer' – can cause problems, especially if you have to look for it in the dictionary.
> **Partout** – 'everywhere' – is similar. Easy if you know it but difficult to look up as there are so many options to choose from.
> The last option is not really part of the answer but it does make sense as an answer to this question so you will get a mark for it.

Total marks: 10

Text 3

a. Why did they take the plane at the start of their holiday?   1

To meet up with the other passengers (1)

Clue word: L'avion – aeroplane

> **HINT** Most of the part of the passage for this answer is made up of words you should already have met in class. The one word that might trip you up is **rejoindre** – 'to meet'.

b. What did they think of all there was to do when they first got on the boat?   1

They thought it was incredible (1)

Clue words: Sur le bateau – on the boat

c. What were some of the activities that could be done on the boat besides the cinema? Give two examples.   2

Games rooms/several swimming pools/a weights room (1) AND/OR

Seeing/going to shows in the theatre (1) AND/OR

Organised games for all ages (1)

Clue words: Il y avait – there was

> **HINT** There is nothing in the answer to trip you up. There is a list of activities and you only need to give two of them to get the marks. There are a few extra details you need so make sure you put in all the details in the answer.

d. What did they do when the boat stopped in port?   3

They went into the nearest town (1)

They visited monuments (1)

They went to the shops to buy presents (1)

Clue words: Le bateau faisait escale – the boat stopped

> **HINT** This is a simple list of things they did. Make sure you include **la plus proche** – 'the nearest'; also, the reason why they went to the shops – to buy presents.

e. What did Antoine think of the holiday?   2

It was the best holiday (singular) of his life (1)

Antoine hopes his parents <u>will</u> organise another cruise next year (1)

Clue words: À vrai dire – it is true to say

> **HINT** In the French the word for 'holiday' is plural and in English it is singular. You must show this in your answer. This is also testing that you have understood the future tense – **mes parents organiseront** – 'my parents will organise'.

f.   Why has Antoine written this article? Tick one box.   **1**

To advertise cruises	
To tell you about his holiday last year	✓
To warn you against going on a cruise	

> **HINT** Read the whole article. Decide what the purpose of the article is. This question is straightforward and, although you need to think about the passage, there is usually one option you can disregard. Look at the other two and decide which would best sum up what the whole passage is about. Sometimes it helps to think which one would be the best title for the passage.

Total marks: 10

Listening – Answer Scheme (20 marks)

Passage 1

Françoise tells you about her experience of going to secondary school in France.

a.   Where did Francoise go to primary school?   **2**

She went to primary in the next village (1)

She took the (school) bus (1)

> **HINT** Listen out for **l'école primaire** – 'primary school' – as that will let you know where the answer is. You need to put in that it was in the next village – which you can get from **voisin** – meaning 'neighbouring'. You don't need to say that it was the school bus – the bus on its own will do.

b.   When did things change?   **1**

When she went to lycée/secondary school (1)

> **HINT** The answer is mentioned twice, even if you don't get all the details around it in the passage. Listen out for **changé** – 'changed' – as the English and French are alike.

c.   Why did she have to spend the week staying at school?   **1**

There was not a lycée/secondary school near her house (1)

> **HINT** Even if you put the answer 'the lycée was too far' you would still get the mark. You do not need to translate the passage exactly – just give the same idea as the answer.

d. When did she return home? 1

On Saturday at midday/after spending the morning at school (1)

> *HINT* There are two answers and you only need to pick one. One of the answers is really straightforward, but you must include the time. The other is more complicated but you do not need to be exact in your answer.

e. What did she do during the week? Give one example. 1

She did her homework (1) AND/OR

She had a lot of homework to do (1) AND/OR

She had a lot of biology/maths homework to do (1)

> *HINT* You only need to write one of these answers to get the mark. Although the last one contains all the detail, you do not need all of this to get a mark.

f. Why did it help her to be staying in school? 1

When she had problems she could go to supported study classes (1) AND/OR

Classes (at the end of the day) (1)

> *HINT* If you don't know the phrase for 'supported study' – **les cours de soutien** – then you should recognise the words for 'the end of the day' and you will get a mark for either.

g. Why is Françoise telling you about this? Tick one box. 1

To tell you about boarding at school during the week in France	✓
To tell you about living in the country in France	
To tell you about school in France	

> *HINT* Listen to the whole article. Decide what the purpose of the article is. This question is straightforward and, although you need to think about the passage, there is usually one option you can disregard. Look at the other two and decide which would best sum up what the whole passage is about. Sometimes it helps to think which one would be the best title for the passage.

Total marks: 8

Passage 2

You then hear your French friend Catherine ask another friend, Guillaume, about going to school in France.

a. What did Guillaume like about going to primary school? Give two examples.   **2**

He got on well with his classmates (1) AND/OR

He had good teachers (1) AND/OR

The food in school was delicious (1)

> *HINT*   It is easier to pinpoint where the correct information is in the second passage as often they follow question/answer. The answers for this question are all in the first answer in the recording. You should have met a lot of the vocabulary in class.

b. What was different about his next school?   **2**

It was in Switzerland/he had moved to Switzerland (1)

He studied (French and maths) and German and English (too) (1)

> *HINT*   The answer for the first part is straightforward. For the second point, make sure that you don't get confused between countries and languages.

c. What was good about moving back to Paris?   **2**

He met up with his old friends (1)

He was very happy (1)

> *HINT*   Don't be confused with the adjective **ancien** – in this case it means 'former' or 'old' – not 'ancient'.

d. Why was he happiest at lycée? Give two examples.   **2**

He did the subjects he wanted (1) AND/OR

He liked his independence (1) AND/OR

He had a lot of work (1) AND/OR

He was able to go out with his friends (1)

> *HINT*   There are four possible answers, so listen carefully to make sure you separate them out into four different points. If you mix them up, you will not get the marks. You only need to put two but if you are not sure put down as much information as you can.

e. What does he want to do after school? Complete the sentence.   **2**

He wants to pass all his exams then <u>work</u> (1) for two or three years and <u>travel</u> (1) a little.

> *HINT*   There are three verbs in this answer that come up a lot but can cause problems: **réussir** – 'to pass'; **travailler** – 'to work'; and **voyager** – 'to travel'. In an exam, students sometimes get these mixed up.

f. **Does he want to continue his studies?** 1

Yes but not straightaway (1)

> *HINT* To answer this you will need to know the phrase **tout de suite** – straight away.

g. **What does he want to study? Give one example.** 1

He is not sure (1) AND/OR

He wants to wait a few years before going to university (1)

> *HINT* You must be able to understand **attendre** – 'to wait' – to understand this part of the answer. Make sure you think carefully about your answer.

Total marks: 12